Pebble Plus

The
U.S. Presidency

by Mari Schuh

Consulting Editor: Gail Saunders-Smith, PhD

Consultant: Steven S. Smith, Kate M. Gregg Distinguished Professor
of Social Sciences and Professor of Political Science
Director, Weidenbaum Center on the Economy, Government, and Public Policy
Washington University, St. Louis, Missouri

CAPSTONE PRESS
a capstone imprint

Pebble Plus is published by Capstone Press,
1710 Roe Crest Drive, North Mankato, Minnesota 56003.
www.capstonepub.com

Books published by Capstone Press are manufactured with paper containing at least 10 percent post-consumer waste.

Library of Congress Cataloging-in-Publication Data
Schuh, Mari C., 1975–
  The U.S. presidency / by Mari Schuh.
     p. cm.—(Pebble plus. The U.S. government)
  Includes bibliographical references and index.
  Summary: "Simple text and full-color photographs provide a brief introduction to the U.S. Presidency"—Provided by publisher.
  ISBN 978-1-4296-7566-6 (library binding)
  1. Presidents—United States—Juvenile literature. I. Title. II. Title: US presidency. III. Title: United States presidency.
  JK517.S26 2012
  352.230973—dc23   2011021662

Editorial Credits

Erika L. Shores, editor; Ashlee Suker, designer; Kathy McColley, production specialist

Photo Credits

Getty Images/AFP/Tim Clary, 13; Alex Wong, 19; Kevin Dietsch, 17
newscom/SHNS photo by Paul Morse/The White House, 7; SIPA/Jim West, 11
Official White House photo by Pete Souza, cover, 5, 15
Shutterstock/Vacclav, 1
U.S. Army photo by Sgt. David House, 21
Wikimedia/whitehouse.gov/Lawrence Jackson, 9

Artistic Effects

Shutterstock: Christophe BOISSON

The author dedicates this book to the memory of her college roommate, Becky Budworth.

Note to Parents and Teachers

The U.S. Government series supports national history standards related to understanding the importance of and basic principles of American democracy. This book describes and illustrates the U.S. presidency. The images support early readers in understanding the text. The repetition of words and phrases helps early readers learn new words. This book also introduces early readers to subject-specific vocabulary words, which are defined in the Glossary section. Early readers may need assistance to read some words and to use the Table of Contents, Glossary, Read More, Internet Sites, and Index sections of the book.

Printed in the United States of America in North Mankato, Minnesota.
102011   006405CGS12

Table of Contents

Leading the United States

The president is the leader
of the United States.
The president has one
of the most important jobs
in the world.

Three Branches

The U.S. government has three branches. The president leads the executive branch. This branch puts laws into effect and makes sure people follow them.

Congress is the legislative

branch. It makes laws.

Courts are the judicial branch.

Courts explain the laws.

IN GOD WE TRUST

Becoming President

People vote for presidents

in elections. Presidents serve

for a term of four years.

A president can be elected

two times.

Polls Open 7:00 am   Polls Close 8:00 pm

VOTE
HERE

City Clerk

Janice M. Winfrey

Presidents must be born in the United States. They must have lived in the United States for 14 years or more. They need to be at least 35 years old.

Working as President

The president lives and
works in the White House
in Washington, D.C.
The president's office is called
the Oval Office.

The president's cabinet members give the president advice. Cabinet members lead health, education, and other departments.

President George W. Bush and cabinet members

17

Presidents work hard

for the people of the United States.

Presidents meet with leaders

from other countries.

Presidents lead the military
and also sign bills into law.
Presidents make difficult decisions
every day.

Glossary

bill—a written plan for a new law; the president signs bills to make them laws

cabinet—a group of government leaders that gives the president advice; cabinet members lead 15 major government departments; the vice president is also a member of the cabinet

Congress—the part of the U.S. government that makes laws; Congress makes up the legislative branch of government

courts—the part of the U.S. government that explains the laws; courts make up the judicial branch of the government

election—the process of choosing someone or deciding something for office by voting

law—a rule made by the government that must be obeyed; Congress makes laws

military—the armed forces of a country

term—a set period of time that elected leaders serve in office

Read More

Gorman, Jacqueline Laks. *President.* Know Your Government. Pleasantville, N.Y.: Weekly Reader, 2009.

Jakubiak, David J. *What Does the President Do?* How Our Government Works. New York: PowerKids Press, 2010.

Rissman, Rebecca. *Presidents' Day.* Holidays and Festivals. Chicago: Heinemann Library, 2011.

Internet Sites

FactHound offers a safe, fun way to find Internet sites related to this book. All of the sites on FactHound have been researched by our staff.

Here's all you do:

Visit *www.facthound.com*

Type in this code: 9781429675666

Super-cool stuff!

Check out projects, games and lots more at www.capstonekids.com

Index

Word Count: 182

Grade: 1

Early-Intervention Level: 20